THE PEARSON PAPERS

PAPER NUMBER 3

AFRICAN PEACEKEEPERS:

PARTNERS OR PROXIES?

Modern international stability operations frequently involve several warring factions, an unstable or non-existent truce and a national theatre of operations. To deal with these operations there is a *New Peacekeeping Partnership:* The ***New Peacekeeping Partnership*** is the term applied to those organizations and individuals that work together to improve the effectiveness of modern peacekeeping operations. It includes the military; civil police; government and non-government agencies dealing with human rights and humanitarian assistance; diplomats; the media; and organizations sponsoring development and democratization programmes. The Pearson Peacekeeping Centre serves the *New Peacekeeping Partnership* by providing national and international participants with the opportunity to examine specific peacekeeping issues, and to update their knowledge of the latest peacekeeping practices.

Canadian Cataloguing in Publication Data

Berman, Eric

    African peacekeepers

    (The Pearson papers; 3)

    Includes bibliographical references.

    ISBN 1-896551-21-1

1. Conflict management -- Africa. 2. International police. 3. National security -- Africa. 4. Organization of African Unity -- Armed forces. 5. Economic Community of West African States -- Armed forces. I. Sams, Katie E., 1969- II. Title. III. Series.

KZ6376.B47 1998   341.5'84'096   C98-950265-1

Printed by Brown Book Company Ltd., Toronto, ON

BY ERIC G. BERMAN
AND KATIE E. SAMS

THE PEARSON PAPERS

PAPER NUMBER 3

AFRICAN PEACEKEEPERS:
PARTNERS OR PROXIES?

The Canadian Peacekeeping Press

1998

The Lester B. Pearson
Canadian International Peacekeeping
Training Centre
President, Alex Morrison, MSC. CD. MA

The Pearson Peacekeeping Centre supports and enhances the Canadian contribution to international peace, security, and stability. The Centre conducts research and provides advanced training and educational programmes, and is a division of the Canadian Institute of Strategic Studies. The Canadian Peacekeeping Press is the publishing division of the Pearson Peacekeeping Centre.

Canadian Peacekeeping Press publications include:

Peacekeeping at a Crossroads (1997)

Refugees, Resources and Resoluteness (1997)

Multilateralism and Regional Security (1997)

Theory, Doctrine and Practice
of Conflict De-Escalation in Peacekeeping Operations (1997)

Facing the Future:
Proceedings of the 1996 Canada-Japan Conference on Modern Peacekeeping
(1997)

Peacekeeping with Muscle (1997)

Seeds of Freedom:
Personal Reflections on the Dawning of Democracy (1996)

Analytic Approaches to the Study of Future Conflict (1996)

The Centre-Periphery Debate in International Security (1996)

Rapid Reaction Capabilities: Requirements and Prospects
*Les capacités de réaction rapide de l'ONU:
exigences et perspectives* (1996)

The New Peacekeeping Partnership (1995)

For publications information, please contact:

Sue Armstrong, Director of Publications and Production
The Pearson Peacekeeping Centre
Cornwallis Park, PO Box 100
Clementsport, NS B0S 1E0 CANADA
Tel: (902) 638-8611 ext. 161 Fax: (902) 638-8576
E-mail: sarmstro@ppc.cdnpeacekeeping.ns.ca

Or visit the Pearson Peacekeeping Centre website:
http://www.cdnpeacekeeping.ns.ca

The Centre (a division of the Canadian Institute of Strategic Studies), established by the Government of Canada in 1994, is funded, in part, by the Department of Foreign Affairs and International Trade and the Department of National Defence of Canada.

Le centre (une division de l'Institut canadien d'études stratégiques) à été établi par le Gouvernement du Canada en 1994. Le soutien financier de Centre provient, en partie, des ministères des Affaires étrangères et du commerce international et de la Défense nationale.

Table of Contents

About the Authors

Eric G. Berman is currently based in Nairobi, where he is the Political Affairs Officer for the UN International Commission of Inquiry (Rwanda). His previous UN experience includes serving as the Assistant Spokesman for the UN Transitional Authority in Cambodia (UNTAC) and as the Special Assistant to the Director-General of the UN Office at Geneva. He was subsequently Executive Director of UN Watch, a non-governmental organization based in Geneva. He undertook this research with Ms. Sams while he was a Visiting Researcher at the United Nations Institute for Disarmament Research in Geneva and the Institute for Security Studies in Halfway House, South Africa.

His published work includes, "The Security Council's Increasing Reliance on Burden-Sharing: Collaboration or Abrogation?," in *International Peacekeeping*, Vol. 4, No. 1, Spring 1998; "Bringing New Life to UN Human Rights Operations," (New York: United Nations Association of the United States of America, January 1998), and "Managing Arms in Peace Processes: Mozambique," (Geneva: United Nations Institute for Disarmament Research, 1996).

Mr. Berman received a Master's degree in International Relations from Yale University and a Bachelor's degree in Political Science from the University of Michigan, Ann Arbor.

Katie E. Sams is a Research Fellow at the United Nations Institute for Disarmament Research in Geneva and is writing a monograph on peacekeeping in Africa. She is also a Visiting Researcher at the Institute for Security Studies in Halfway House, South Africa. Previously, she was a Researcher at UN Watch in Geneva. She has election monitoring experience with the Organization for Security and Co-operation in Europe in Bosnia and Herzegovina, and with the International Commission of Jurists in Madagascar.

Ms. Sams received a Master's degree in International Relations from the Graduate Institute of International Studies in Geneva, a *Juris Doctor* degree from the Georgetown University Law Center, and a Bachelor's degree in English and French from Dartmouth College. She is a member of the New York Bar.

Acknowledgement

This article is based on a paper presented at the eleventh annual meeting of the Academic Council on the United Nations System (ACUNS) in Cornwallis, Nova Scotia on 18 June 1998 and is current as of 1 July 1998. The authors would like to thank the Lester B. Pearson Canadian International Peacekeeping Training Centre for its generous financial assistance, which enabled them to attend and participate in the ACUNS conference. This article is part of an ongoing research and writing project on African peacekeeping, which will culminate in a book published by the United Nations Institute for Disarmament Research in Geneva, Switzerland, and the Institute for Security Studies in Halfway House, South Africa. The authors would also like to thank the Geneva Foundation to Protect Health in War for its financial support.

Introduction

During their recent visits to Africa, United Nations Secretary-General Kofi Annan and United States President Bill Clinton acknowledged the international community's past failure to summon the political will or the financial and human resources to respond meaningfully to African conflicts. They sought to convince Africa that the international community has learned from its previous mistakes. Skeptical of these assurances, African countries are attempting to become more self-reliant.

Recent responses to conflicts in the Central African Republic (CAR), the Republic of Congo, and Sierra Leone highlight the inadequacies of the *status quo*. In general, African countries remain very limited in their abilities to respond effectively on their own. They were unable to field a force in CAR or Congo without outside assistance. While Nigeria's ability to deploy a sizeable force in Sierra Leone is impressive, its inability to provide the necessary logistical re-supply and effective command and control to its troops further afield has undermined its effectiveness.

These three examples also suggest that little has changed in the West's fundamental approach to Africa. The international community's (in)action in Congo illustrates the hollowness of Western proclamations about the need to respect the rule of law and the value of free elections. The Security Council failed to act swiftly and with determination to ensure that the democratically-elected government was not overthrown. It proved easy for the Council to forcefully condemn the military coup in Sierra Leone because no further commitment was required of it. Unwilling to act itself, the Council welcomed the Nigerian intervention despite its obvious ironies. The CAR case highlights that cooperation among Western countries is selective and inconsistent.

The West -- and by extension the Security Council -- is still pursuing "disengagement" policies. Current Western "capacity-building" initiatives, which ostensibly aim to build a partnership between the West and Africa, will also enable Western countries to avoid becoming directly engaged on the front lines. The Security Council has embraced Chapter VIII of the UN Charter, which authorizes it to share the burden of maintaining international peace and security, for selfish reasons and not for the greater good. Too often, the Council has relied on proxies whose motives or insufficient capabilities have served to further jeopardize international peace and security, rather than to promote it.

Partly in response to perceived Western indifference, African states have begun to exhibit a growing political willingness to intervene -- through regional and sub-regional organizations and *ad hoc* coalitions -- in African conflicts. (Unilateral efforts are still viewed with suspicion.) Whereas even talk of such interference into a state's internal affairs was once considered taboo, there has been a noticeable shift away from the traditional respect for sovereignty. In addition to political censure and other diplomatic measures, economic and military responses are increasingly considered appropriate tools.

While it is important that African regional and sub-regional actors have recognized the need to take primary responsibility for responding to crises, their ability to undertake credible and effective peacekeeping operations remains limited. The Organization of African Unity (OAU) has shown itself more adept at creating institutional mechanisms than at fielding operations that respond meaningfully. Of the various sub-regional organizations on the continent, only the Economic Community of West African States (ECOWAS) has been able to deploy a sizeable military force. As its involvement in Liberia illustrates, however, numbers alone do not make a force credible or effective. Several *ad hoc* coalitions also show the present limitations of African peacekeeping and peace enforcement arrangements.

This paper examines current efforts to develop African capacities to undertake peacekeeping and peace enforcement operations. It describes various Western capacity-building initiatives and African attempts to manage and resolve conflicts on their continent. It then highlights the incongruities between Western "largesse" and African needs. The paper concludes that despite current Western and African efforts, the factors resulting in inaction four years ago in Rwanda still persist.

Western Responses

Partly in recognition of African countries' limited capabilities -- and partly in an effort to avoid being drawn into the conflicts themselves -- a number of Western states have begun to pursue similar policies to redress these shortcomings. France, the United Kingdom, and the United States have taken the lead in this regard. In May 1997, they announced a common capacity-building policy, which they termed the "P-3 Initiative."[1] Through this program the three countries sought not only to coordinate and strengthen their individual policies, but to provide a forum in which other countries already providing support or wishing to do so could participate.

The desire to enhance African peacekeeping capabilities predates the P-3 Initiative. In November 1995, UN Secretary-General Boutros Boutros-Ghali submitted a report entitled *Improving preparedness for conflict prevention and peace-keeping in Africa.*[2] The document was a useful starting point for developing much-needed political support to strengthen African peacekeeping, but it suggested only "modest" measures.

The 5 December 1997 meeting at UN Headquarters spawned by the P-3 highlighted the plethora of undertakings already in existence. They ranged from convening small, one-time, conflict-prevention seminars to sustained multi-year peacekeeping training as well as from distributing syllabi in the classroom to military equipment in the field. Fifteen Western countries shared information on their various programs.[3]

United Kingdom

The UK African Peacekeeping Training Support Programme is multifaceted. An important component of the British program is developing the Army Staff

---

[1] Prior to May 1997 and the P-3 Initiative, France and the United Kingdom had cooperated bilaterally and through the Western European Union.

[2] See A/50/711 - S/1995/911, 1 November 1995.

[3] Denmark's program to strengthen the Zimbabwe Staff College's role as a Regional Peacekeeping Centre is particularly ambitious. The initial budget for the three-year program was roughly US$ 900,000 per year. Memorandum of Understanding between Denmark and Zimbabwe, 31 January 1997, courtesy of the Royal Danish Embassy, Harare.

Colleges of Ghana and Zimbabwe into regional peacekeeping training centers. British Military Advisory and Training Teams (BMATTs) are based in Accra and Harare and provide training to the host countries as well as other African states. Ghanaian and Zimbabwean troops received BMATT training prior to deploying to Liberia and Angola, respectively.[4] The British and Ugandan governments recently signed a memorandum of understanding on the establishment of a third BMATT in Kampala.[5]

Besides providing bilateral assistance, the UK has also aided sub-regional initiatives. In April 1997, it supported a three-week peacekeeping exercise hosted by Zimbabwe, which was known as *Blue Hungwe*. Some 1,600 troops from 10 African countries within the Southern African Development Community (SADC) participated in the exercise.[6] The UK has offered to assist the upcoming sub-regional peacekeeping exercise, *Blue Crane,* which South Africa will host in November 1998. It has also expressed a desire to support a regional peacekeeping exercise for West Africa in 1999.[7]

The UK has supported and initiated several other projects designed to strengthen African peacekeeping. Together with Nigeria, it co-chaired an informal working group that produced a paper entitled *Conflict Prevention and Peace-keeping in Africa*, which was submitted to the Secretaries-General of the UN and the OAU in April 1995. (The aforementioned November 1995 Report by Boutros-Ghali borrowed heavily from this work.) In an effort to promote anglophone/francophone military cooperation in theater, the UK funded an English/French peacekeeping dictionary produced jointly by the Ghanaian and Senegalese armed forces. It has sponsored the secondment of African officers to the UN Department of Peacekeeping Operations in New York as well.

France

The centerpiece of France's policy, *Renforcement des capacités africaines de maintien de la paix* (RECAMP), offers training, equipment, and instruction. France's previous proposal to establish a standing African peacekeeping force never received

---

[4] Statement made by Alice Walpole, Head, Peacekeeping Section, United Nations Department of the British Foreign and Commonwealth Office, Institute for Security Studies Peacekeeping Seminar, Halfway House, South Africa, 5 November 1997.

[5] Telephone interview with Gill Coglin, Acting Head, Peacekeeping Section, United Nations Department of the British Foreign and Commonwealth Office, 23 July 1998.

[6] SADC members Mauritius and Zambia did not participate. Slightly more than half of the 1,584 troops were from Zimbabwe. Angola sent only two civilian police, and Botswana sent only two civilian police and two observers. Interview with Brigadier Adrian Naughten, Commander of BMATT Southern Africa, Harare, 26 January 1998, and written correspondence of 9 February 1998. (Democratic Republic of Congo (DRC) and Seychelles, SADC's most recent members, did not join the sub-regional organization until after *Blue Hungwe*.)

[7] Statement made by Rosalind Marsden, Head, United Nations Department of the British Foreign and Commonwealth Office, Meeting on Enhancing African Capacity for Peacekeeping, New York, 5 December 1997.

much support from within the French government, let alone from African countries or the international community. In the wake of the controversies surrounding the French-led "humanitarian" force in Rwanda, *Operation Turquoise,* it was not an opportune time politically to sell such a concept. Rather than creating a standing force, RECAMP aims to develop "standby force modules" that can be called upon to participate in UN- and OAU-authorized operations.[8]

The first training under RECAMP was held in February 1998 in Senegal. The exercise, called *Guidimakha,* built upon a more modest multinational undertaking held in Togo in March 1997.[9] Some 3,600 troops from 11 African and Western countries[10] took part in the 10-day exercise. Mali, Mauritania, and Senegal each were represented at battalion strength. Five other African countries provided platoons: Cape Verde, Gambia, Ghana, Guinea, and Guinea Bissau. France supplied roughly 900 troops. The UK and the US also provided small contingents. France intends to support future African sub-regional exercises every two years.

France also used *Guidimakha* as an occasion to pre-position equipment in Dakar, for use in the exercise as well as in future peacekeeping operations. The equipment will remain the property of France and under French control. France will also assume responsibility for maintaining it. After *Guidimakha,* France left behind approximately 140 vehicles as well as a field hospital.[11] Much of this equipment has subsequently been used to support the UN peacekeeping force in the Central African Republic. France plans to pre-position additional equipment over the next two years in other African countries and sub-regions.[12]

Under RECAMP, France also plans to provide additional peacekeeping instruction. It has long opened participation in courses conducted at its military staff colleges to African officers. In addition, France provides financial assistance to five African national military staff colleges, which have been designated to provide training to other nationals as well.[13] Although these centers focus on basic military *savoir faire,* they include peacekeeping modules. Together with Côte d'Ivoire, France is also establishing a regional peacekeeping training center outside Yamoussoukro, which will open in 1999.[14] Initially, training will be offered to West

---

[8] Statement of France, Meeting on Enhancing African Capacity for Peacekeeping, New York, 5 December 1997.

[9] Some 4,000 troops from Benin, Burkina Faso, France, and Togo took part in the week-long *Nangbeto* exercise.

[10] Belgium provided a C-130 aircraft but no troops and therefore is not included in this number.

[11] Interviews with French military officials at *Guidimakha,* Dakar and Bakel, Senegal, 23-28 February 1998.

[12] Interviews with French military and diplomatic officials, Paris, 28-29 May 1998.

[13] These schools are located in Côte d'Ivoire, Mali, Mauritania, Senegal, and Togo.

[14] The construction of the center will cost France around US$ 3 million, and France will also provide a monthly allowance to participants. Interview with Col. Jacques Digonnet, Deputy Chief, Military Cooperation Mission, French Ministry of Cooperation, Paris, 29 May 1998.

African participants, but the program will be expanded to include others from outside of the sub-region. Each course will comprise around 40 officers.[15]

United States

The US African Crisis Response Initiative (ACRI) provides recipients with classical peacekeeping training and related equipment.[16] Initially, ACRI was known as the African Crisis Response Force (ACRF). The name change occurred in response to unanticipated stiff resistance by African leaders. It is not simply cosmetic. Whereas very little thought had gone into ACRF,[17] considerably more planning has gone into ACRI.[18] Training commenced in July 1997, and the intention is to have some 10 battalions trained within the next five years.[19]

The program is divided into two "phases." Phase 1 provides basic soldier skills to troops at the battalion level over a two-month period. Under the rationale that a good peacekeeper must first be a good soldier, the program includes marksmanship training. The importance of developing and maintaining good relations with civil society is also stressed. Phase 2 encompasses six shorter "Sustainment Training" modules to take place at six-month intervals.[20]

ACRI also provides equipment for the soldier and the battalion. Each trainee is outfitted with a complete uniform, personal gear, and even eyeglasses if necessary.[21] Provision is made for communications equipment (US radios and British repeaters), night vision binoculars (Russian), and mine detectors (Austrian). Emphasizing inter-operability, the US supplies recipients with equipment that meets UN specifications whenever possible. Except for small arms ammunition used for marksmanship training, ACRI does not include any lethal equipment.

---

[15] *Ibid.*

[16] The US has numerous other bilateral and multilateral military assistance programs, many of which include peacekeeping components. However, because peacekeeping is not their primary focus, they are not addressed in this paper.

[17] As one US military officer familiar with the program said bluntly, the planning behind ACRF was "no more thought out than the briefing slides handed out." Interview with US government official, Washington, DC, 12 March 1998.

[18] For an analysis of ACRI's origins, shortcomings, and potential, see Dan Henk and Steven Metz, *The United States and the Transformation of African Security: The African Crisis Response Initiative and Beyond*, Carlisle, Pennsylvania: Strategic Studies Institute, US Army War College, 5 December 1997.

[19] The American diplomat heading ACRI speaks of the desirability of training 10 - 14 battalions and 10 - 12,000 troops. Interview with Amb. Marshall Fletcher McCallie, Special Coordinator of the African Crisis Response Initiative's Interagency Working Group, Washington, DC, 10 March 1998.

[20] Interview with Maj. Richard Naughton, Office of the Deputy Assistant Secretary of Defense for Peacekeeping and Peace Enforcement Policy, the Pentagon, 11 March 1998.

[21] Col. David E. McCracken, "On the Record Briefing," Amb. Marshall F. McCallie and Col. David E. McCracken, US Department of State, Washington, DC, 28 July 1997.

To date, six African countries have concluded agreements with the US.[22] Senegal and Uganda were the first to receive training (beginning in July 1997), followed by Malawi (September 1997), Mali (February 1998), and Ghana (April 1998). Ethiopia was scheduled to receive training in the second half of 1998, but that training has been put on hold because of recent hostilities between Ethiopia and Eritrea and will be reassessed.[23] Unlike the other recipients, Ethiopia was to have not one but two infantry battalions trained under the program. It was also to provide a headquarters unit. Phase two training has already commenced with Senegal and Uganda.

[22] Tunisia had been one of the initial seven countries tentatively selected to receive ACRI training, but made too many demands (such as the provision of armored vehicles). Interview with Charles Ikins, Management Consultant, Cohen and Woods International, Arlington, Virginia, 11 March 1998.

[23] Telephone interview with Lt. Col. Michael Bailey, Chief Operating Officer, Office of Peacekeeping and Humanitarian Operations, US Department of Defense, 20 August 1998.

African Responses

Many African states fear that these capacity-building initiatives are a manifestation of Western disengagement.[24] This concern partly explains why several have distanced themselves from ACRI. While a number of African countries have participated in Western-sponsored bilateral and sub-regional training programs, no African regional or sub-regional organization has formally approved of Western capacity-building initiatives.[25]

Aware of the West's ambivalence, Africans have begun to take primary responsibility for resolving problems on their continent. They are attempting to become more self-sufficient in responding militarily to various crises by developing collective responses. Toward this end, a number of political and economic alliances on the African continent have been expanded to include military dimensions. The OAU and various African sub-regional organizations are attempting to create new mechanisms and develop new capabilities. African states are also increasingly willing to form *ad hoc* coalitions to respond to conflicts.

OAU

The establishment of the Mechanism for Conflict Prevention, Management and Resolution is a partial response by the OAU to fears of Africa's marginalization in the post-Cold War era.[26] Formally adopted at the OAU Cairo Summit in June 1993,

---

[24] For some, it is not simply a question of disengagement. Nigeria has been particularly critical of the P-3 Initiative. Its foreign minister, for example, has characterized the undertaking as divisive and designed to carve out spheres of influence. While Nigeria is not a disinterested observer (under its present military leadership it cannot be considered for ACRI training), several other countries reportedly supported Nigeria's strong stand at the OAU Council of Ministers Meeting in February 1998. Various media reports listed Kenya, South Africa, and Zimbabwe, in addition to Libya and Sudan, as having supported Nigeria at the meeting. See, for example, Ghion Hagos, "Nigeria Leads African Opposition to Western Peace Force Plan," *Panafrican News Agency*, 1 March 1998.

[25] At a November 1997 ambassadorial-level meeting, the OAU Central Organ simply "took note" of the various initiatives aimed at enhancing African capacities in a communiqué. The February 1998 OAU Council of Ministers Meeting also "took note" of the initiatives, instead of offering its "support," as had appeared in an earlier draft of the decision. *Ibid.*

[26] See Makumi Mwagiru, "The Organization of African Unity and the Management of Internal Conflicts in Africa," *International Studies*, Vol. 3, No. 1, January - March 1996, p.7.

the Mechanism owes its origins to the July 1990 *Declaration of the Heads of State and Government of the OAU on the Political and Socio-Economic Situation in Africa and the Fundamental Changes Taking Place in the World.* The Mechanism represents an important change in the organization's willingness to intervene on issues of sovereignty that might previously have been deemed "off-limits."[27] It provides the OAU Secretary-General with greater flexibility to undertake initiatives concerning "internal" affairs of OAU member states.

The Mechanism is just one of several recent OAU developments intended to strengthen its ability to promote peace and security. A Peace Fund has been created to provide regular and continuous support for activities relating to conflict management and resolution. The OAU has also established a Conflict Management Centre (CMC), which houses the Mechanism's secretariat -- the Conflict Management Division. CMC activity centers around a Crisis Management Room -- a 24-hour situation room where civilians and military officers will monitor crises in Africa. The CMC also comprises an Early Warning Network designed to facilitate the exchange of information. An important component of this Network is a database that contains information on OAU member states and their capabilities.[28]

Moreover, in recent years, the OAU has established peacekeeping operations in three conflicts.[29] The first, the Neutral Military Observer Group (NMOG) in Rwanda, was authorized in July 1992, prior to the Mechanism's creation. In August 1993, the Mechanism approved NMOG II. The Observer Mission in Burundi (OMIB) was established in April 1994. In December 1997, the OAU dispatched an observer group to the Comoros.[30]

The OAU has also taken preliminary steps toward establishing a standby African peacekeeping force. The OAU Council of Ministers first recommended that OAU member states identify ready contingents on a voluntary basis to serve in UN or, exceptionally, OAU missions in 1995.[31] In June 1996, the Chiefs of Defence

---

[27] Four principles have traditionally guided OAU conflict management: (1) non-interference in the internal affairs of states, (2) the sovereign equality of member states; (3) the respect of the territorial integrity of member states; and (4) the principle of "African solutions to African problems." *Ibid.,* p.5.

[28] Telephone interview with William Nhara, Co-ordinator for Conflict Prevention and Research, OAU Conflict Management Division, 20 August 1998. See also William Nhara, "The OAU and the Potential Role of Regional and Sub-Regional Organisations," in Jakkie Cilliers and Greg Mills, eds., *Peacekeeping in Africa. Vol. 2,* Halfway House, South Africa: Institute for Defence Policy, 1996, p.107.

[29] The OAU's only previous foray into peacekeeping was in Chad in 1981.

[30] The OAU also had indicated its willingness to provide civilian observers to assist in overseeing the referendum in Western Sahara. However, Morocco, which withdrew from the OAU when the organization recognized the Saharoui Arab Democratic Republic, refused to consider OAU participation.

[31] OAU Secretary-General Salim Ahmed Salim first spoke of the need for every OAU member state to earmark a contingent that could be called upon to respond to African conflicts in 1992. He indicated that these contingents should train together in order to familiarize themselves with one another and their respective equipment. Interview with Chris J. Bakwesegha, Assistant Executive Secretary for Political Affairs, Permanent Observer Mission of the Organization of African Unity to the United Nations, New York, 13 March 1998.

Staff of member states of the OAU Central Organ examined this issue and concurred. During their second meeting, in October 1997, the Chiefs of Defence Staff recommended that the OAU could earmark a brigade-sized contribution to standby arrangements from each of the five African sub-regions. They also suggested that the OAU should identify 100 military and civilian observers from each of the sub-regions as a starting point.[32] In March 1998, the Council of Ministers agreed that an eventual African peacekeeping force should be made up of sub-regional brigades under the OAU's command and control, within the framework of the OAU Central Organ.[33]

African Sub-regional Organizations

All of these OAU initiatives are intended to complement the expanding efforts of sub-regional organizations. Several African sub-regional groupings have recently established peace and security frameworks and have begun to develop peacekeeping structures. The Economic Community of West African States and the Southern African Development Community have made particular progress in these directions and are discussed separately below. In 1990, the Arab Maghreb Union (AMU)[34] established an informal organ known as the Council for Common Defense. In 1992, the Economic Community of Central African States (ECCAS)[35] established -- through the UN -- a *Standing Advisory Committee on Security Matters in Central Africa* and subsequently has concluded a non-aggression pact and undertaken initial joint military training in preparation for possible joint peace operations. In 1994, the Inter-Governmental Authority on Development (IGAD)[36] expanded its mandate to include a mediating role in the Sudanese conflict, and has since tried its hand in Somalia. In April 1997, the Treaty of Non-Aggression, Assistance and Mutual Defense (known by its French acronym, ANAD)[37] began to investigate the modalities for a sub-regional peacekeeping force in West Africa. Presently, the Commission for East African Co-operation (EAC)[38] has before it a draft treaty to establish the East African Community, which provides a possible basis for joint military

---

[32] See Draft Report of the Second Meeting of the Chiefs of Defence Staff of the Central Organ of the OAU, 24-25 October 1997, OAU/CHST/Co/Draft/Rpt (II).

[33] See "OAU Wants Sub-regional Brigades for African Force," *Panafrican News Agency*, 9 March 1998.

[34] AMU, created in 1989, has five members: Algeria, Libya, Mauritania, Morocco, and Tunisia.

[35] ECCAS, created in 1981, is comprised of the following 11 member states: Angola, Burundi, Cameroon, CAR, Chad, Congo, DRC, Equatorial Guinea, Gabon, Rwanda, and São Tomé and Principe.

[36] IGAD was formerly the Inter-Governmental Authority on Drought and Development (IGADD), which was created in 1986. It has seven members: Djibouti, Eritrea, Ethiopia, Kenya, Somalia, Sudan, and Uganda.

[37] ANAD, created in 1997, has seven member states: Burkina Faso, Côte d'Ivoire, Mali, Mauritania, Niger, Senegal, and Togo. Benin and Guinea are observers.

[38] EAC, which was created in 1966 as the East African Community and collapsed ten years later, was relaunched in its current incarnation in 1996. Its members have always comprised Kenya, Tanzania, and Uganda.

operations,[39] and in June 1998 the three member states (together with the US) undertook their first joint peacekeeping exercise.[40]

ECOWAS [41]

The security dimension of ECOWAS has developed over time, but it was the Liberian civil war that prompted it to intervene militarily to promote peace. ECOWAS member states adopted a *Protocol on Non-Aggression* in 1978 and a *Protocol Relating to Mutual Assistance on Defence* in 1981. The latter document, which entered into force in 1986, created a sub-regional defense body -- the Allied Armed Forces of the Community -- to be comprised of national units from existing armed forces.[42] In response to the Liberian crisis, ECOWAS established a Community Standing Mediation Committee, which created the ECOWAS Cease-fire Monitoring Group (ECOMOG) at its inaugural session.[43] On 24 August 1990, ECOWAS dispatched a 3,500-strong force comprised of troops from five member states. In July 1997, a much larger force oversaw the presidential elections, which formally ended the civil war.[44]

ECOMOG has since deployed in Sierra Leone in support of the democratically-elected government, which fell in a May 1997 *coup d'état*. On 27 August 1997, ECOWAS imposed an embargo on all supplies of arms, military equipment, and petroleum products to Sierra Leone and authorized "sub-regional forces" to ensure its implementation.[45] In February 1998, the Nigerian-led "ECOMOG" force launched an offensive and quickly captured the capital, Freetown, on 13 February 1998.

---

[39] See Articles 131 (Political Affairs), 132 (Regional Peace and Security), and 133 (Defence), "EAC Draft Treaty (Part III)," *The East African*, 1-7 June 1998, p.17.

[40] The exercise, known as *Natural Fire*, comprised approximately 2,000 troops, of which the host, Kenya, provided roughly two-thirds.

[41] ECOWAS, established in 1975, is comprised of 16 member states: Benin, Burkina Faso, Cape Verde, Côte d'Ivoire, Gambia, Ghana, Guinea, Guinea Bissau, Liberia, Mali, Mauritania, Niger, Nigeria, Senegal, Sierra Leone, and Togo.

[42] Article 2, ECOWAS Protocol Relating to Mutual Assistance on Defence, 29 May 1981, reprinted in M. Weller, ed., *Regional Peace-keeping and International Enforcement: the Liberian Crisis*, Cambridge: Cambridge University Press, 1994, p.19.

[43] In 1993, ECOWAS members revised the ECOWAS treaty to reflect the organization's expanded role. Article 58 of the revised treaty explicitly authorizes ECOWAS member states to "establish a regional peace and security observation system and peace-keeping forces where appropriate." Revised Treaty of the Economic Community of West African States, 24 July 1993, reprinted in *International Legal Materials*, Vol. 33, 1993, p.689.

[44] In February 1998, Liberian President Charles Taylor announced that a "capacity-building" force of 4,000 - 5,000 troops would remain in the country to assist with the restructuring of the army and the provision of security. See Tapitapia Sannah, "Mandate of ECOMOG ends," *Panafrican News Agency*, 2 February 1998.

[45] See "Letter dated 8 September 1997 from the Permanent Representative of Nigeria to the Untied Nations addressed to the President of the Security Council (Annex I)," containing "Final Communiqué of the Summit of the Economic Community of West African States, 28 and 29 August 1997," S/1997/695, 8 September 1997. A month later, the UN passed a resolution imposing sanctions against Sierra Leone and authorizing ECOMOG to ensure its implementation. See S/RES/1132 (1997), 8 October 1997.

Since then, ECOMOG has been attempting to secure the countryside.[46]

In July 1998, ECOWAS Defense and Foreign Ministers met in Abidjan and extended ECOMOG's mandate to include Guinea Bissau, but they did not explicitly authorize the use of force. Senegal and Guinea, both members of ECOWAS, have intervened militarily at the request of Guinea Bissau's democratically-elected president, Nino Vieira. The troops, however, do not yet constitute an ECOMOG force.[47]

ECOWAS has recently taken steps to establish a permanent peacekeeping force. In December 1997, ECOWAS Heads of State agreed in principle to set up a formal mechanism to prevent conflict and supervise peacekeeping in the sub-region.[48] In March 1998, a ministerial-level meeting was convened to decide upon the structure of this mechanism. Debate centered around whether ECOMOG should be transformed into a permanent force or whether another peace force should be constituted.[49] The ministers ultimately decided that ECOMOG would serve as the basis for the future peacekeeping body.[50]

SADC [51]

The end of the Cold War and, more directly, the demise of apartheid rule in South Africa, created possibilities for new and enhanced security cooperation among Southern African countries.[52] With the dissolution of the Front Line States (FLS) in July 1994, the need for a mechanism to address defense and security issues in all SADC members became apparent.[53] Reflecting sub-regional consensus on the need for stronger security coordination, SADC created the Organ for Defence, Politics and Security in June 1996 and designated the Inter-State Defence and

---

[46] See "Fourth Report of the Secretary-General on the Situation in Sierra Leone," S/1998/249, 18 March 1998, which describes ECOMOG's concept of operations and outlines its tasks.

[47] Melvis Dzisah, "Ministers Endorse ECOMOG Intervention in Guinea-Bissau," *Panafrican News Agency*, 4 July 1998.

[48] Afeto Kuma, "ECOWAS Extraordinary Summit Ends in Lome," *Panafrican News Agency*, 18 December 1997; see also "West African summit ends," *BBC News*, 17 December 1997.

[49] "News in Brief -- Thursday, 12 March 1998," *Panafrican News Agency*, 12 March 1998.

[50] "West African ministers agree on peacekeeping force," *BBC News*, 13 March 1998.

[51] The organization was known as the Southern African Development Co-ordination Conference (SADCC) from its establishment in 1980 until SADC was created in 1992. SADC is comprised of 14 member states: Angola, Botswana, DRC, Lesotho, Malawi, Mauritius, Mozambique, Namibia, Seychelles, South Africa, Swaziland, Tanzania, Zambia, and Zimbabwe.

[52] See Jakkie Cilliers and Mark Malan, "From destabilization to peace-keeping in Southern Africa," *Africa Insight*, Vol. 26, No. 4, 1996, p.339.

[53] In March 1995, SADC Foreign Ministers recommended that the Association of Southern African States (ASAS) be designated as the primary mechanism for conflict prevention, management, and resolution in Southern Africa. The August 1995 SADC Summit deferred their decision on the issue. J. Cilliers, M. Shaw, and G. Mills, "Towards a Southern African policy on preventive diplomacy and peace support operations," in Mark Shaw and Jakkie Cilliers, eds., *South Africa and Peacekeeping in Africa, Vol. 1*, Halfway House, South Africa: Institute for Defence Policy, 1995, p.5.

Security Committee (ISDSC) as its Secretariat.[54]

The Organ serves as SADC's conflict prevention, management, and resolution body. As such, it is tasked with developing a collective peacekeeping capacity within national armies for use in the sub-region and elsewhere in Africa.[55] Under the ISDSC's supervision, a standby brigade is currently being put together for the sub-region. Each SADC member state is to earmark contingents as well as headquarters staff. The ISDSC has also drawn up a training syllabus for peace support (based on the UN training syllabus) and has designated the Zimbabwe Staff College as the coordinating body for peace support training in the SADC region. In addition, the ISDSC is working to establish a satellite communications system linking the various SADC governments.[56]

Ad Hoc Coalitions

The recent intervention of an inter-African force in the Central African Republic attests to the growing willingness of African states to become involved in neighboring conflicts. Roughly six months after fighting broke out in CAR between troops loyal to President Ange-Félix Patassé and mutinous army officers, the presidents of Burkina Faso, Chad, Gabon, and Mali were asked to mediate a truce between the warring factions. After intensive negotiations, the parties to the conflict signed the Bangui Agreements on 25 January 1997, and created an international committee to monitor their implementation.[57] The four presidents decided to establish the Inter-African Force to Monitor the Implementation of the Bangui Agreements (known by its French acronym, MISAB) following a request from President Patassé. MISAB, deployed in February 1997, was comprised of roughly 800 troops from Burkina Faso, Chad, Gabon, Mali, and later, Senegal and Togo. The Security Council authorized the mission in August 1997.[58] France provided logistical support, and, when necessary, operational backup to MISAB.[59] In April 1998, in view of France's impending withdrawal from the country, the Security Council

---

[54] Prior to 1994, the ISDSC was a sub-structure of the FLS. As such it dealt with the coordination of regional support for the Southern Africa liberation movements. When the SADC Organ was established in 1996, the ISDSC became an institution of the Organ. Interview with Maj-Gen. D.S. Hamman, Secretary, Inter-State Defence and Security Committee, Halfway House, South Africa, 21 January 1998.

[55] See Communiqué issued by the Summit of Heads of State and Government of the Southern African Development Community, Gaborone, Botswana, 28 June 1996.

[56] Interview with Hamman, note 54.

[57] The monitoring committee was comprised of representatives of the four African presidents that had mediated the truce.

[58] See S/RES/1125 (1997), 6 August 1997.

[59] French presence on the ground totalled more than 1,400 troops during the course of the MISAB operation. See "Report of the Secretary-General Pursuant to Resolution 1136 (1997) Concerning the Situation in the Central African Republic," S/1998/61, 23 January 1998, para.28.

established a UN peacekeeping operation to replace the French-supported force.[60]

The still-born peacekeeping initiative in Congo also illustrates the willingness of African states to intervene militarily. Fighting erupted in Congo in June 1997 between the forces of the democratically-elected president, Pascal Lissouba, and the militia of former military ruler, Gen. Denis Sassou-Nguesso. In light of the deteriorating security situation, several of the sub-region's leaders established a mediation committee chaired by President Omar Bongo of Gabon to bring about a peaceful resolution of the crisis. After securing a temporary cease-fire, the committee requested the Security Council to authorize the rapid deployment to Brazzaville of an inter-African force.[61] A number of African states had offered to participate in this force.[62] However, the Council set three preconditions for the establishment of a peacekeeping operation, which were never met. These preconditions were: (1) complete adherence to an agreed and viable cease-fire; (2) agreement to the international control of Brazzaville airport; and (3) a clear commitment to a negotiated settlement covering all political and military aspects of the crisis.[63]

---

[60] See S/RES/1159 (1998), 27 March 1998. The authorized strength of the UN Mission in the Central African Republic (MINURCA) is 1,350. Ten countries are contributing troops: Burkina Faso, Canada, Chad, Côte d'Ivoire, Egypt, France, Gabon, Mali, Senegal, and Togo. France and Canada, the two non-African participants, are providing some 200 and 40 military personnel, respectively.

[61] See "Letter dated 20 June 1997 from the Secretary-General addressed to the President of the Security Council," S/1997/484, 20 June 1997; see also "Letter dated 20 June 1997 from the Secretary-General addressed to the President of the Security Council (Annex)," S/1997/483, 20 June 1997, containing letter dated 16 June 1997 from the President of Gabon addressed to the Secretary-General. President Lissouba as well as OAU Secretary-General Salim Ahmed Salim reiterated this request. See "Letter dated 26 June 1997 from the Secretary-General addressed to the President of the Security Council (Annexes 1 and 2)," S/1997/495, 26 June 1996.

[62] Senegal offered to lead and contribute a battalion to the eventual force. Chad, Mali, and Niger also offered to provide troops. Interview with Lt-Col. Mamadou Dione, Commanding Officer, Senegalese Army Military Academy (Thiès), Dakar, 25 February 1998. See also "Senegal agrees to head Congo intervention force," *Agence France Presse*, 8 July 1997, and "Congo, la situation s'enlise," *Afrique Express* No. 150, 10 July 1997, p.10.

[63] S/PRST/1997/43, 13 August 1997.

Ineffectiveness of Current Approaches

This flurry of diplomatic and military activity, when taken as a whole, appears more significant than it is. The descriptions of the various Western and African undertakings raise important questions about the efficacy of current approaches. There is a significant disparity between Africa's inabilities and needs, on the one hand, and the West's abilities and predisposition on the other. This problem, which the various responses described above purport to address, has long been well-understood.

A Long-Standing and Well-Understood Problem

Difficulties encountered in deploying the United Nations Assistance Mission for Rwanda (UNAMIR) starkly highlighted the problem: as a general rule, African peacekeepers cannot deploy and remain operational without considerable Western assistance, which is often withheld.[64] On 17 May 1994 the Security Council authorized the augmentation of UNAMIR to 5,500 troops.[65] Granted, the three-phase, 31-day deployment plan spelled out in Secretary-General Boutros-Ghali's report to the Council [66] was not realistic. The airport in the capital, Kigali, was too

---

[64] These difficulties also highlighted the questionable utility of the UN Standby Arrangements System. At the time, 19 countries had expressed a willingness to participate in the program, pledging a total of 31,000 military personnel for future operations. When the UN approached them, however, all 19 refused. Mark Malan, "Towards Sounder Investments in Developing African Peace Operations Capabilities," *African Security Review*, Vol. 6, No. 2, 1997, p.17.

[65] Before Rwandan President Juvénal Habyarimana's plane was shot down on 6 April, the force, which comprised 2,165 UN military personnel, was nearly at its fully-authorized strength of 2,548. Fully aware that Tutsis were being slaughtered systematically (and that ten Belgian peacekeepers had been tortured, murdered, and mutilated), the Council decided to *reduce* the force by almost 90 percent to 270. See S/RES/872 (1993), 5 October 1993, and S/RES/912 (1994), 21 April 1994.

[66] "Report of the Secretary-General on the Situation in Rwanda," S/1994/565, 13 May 1994, paras.19-21.

insecure to be utilized.[67] Nevertheless, the French-led *Operation Turquoise* managed to deploy 3,000 troops in the region within days without much difficulty.[68] As of 25 July, ten weeks after the resolution was passed, less than ten percent of the UN force had deployed.[69]

Importantly, the greatest problem lay not with finding (African) countries willing to volunteer troops, although that too took time, but rather with finding (Western) countries willing and able to equip them. Eight states agreed to provide infantry troops -- all from Africa.[70] Five other African countries agreed to provide troops as part of a unified contingent.[71] Boutros-Ghali summed up the situation as follows:

> The deployment of UNAMIR has been a difficult process, as many contingents were in need of major equipment items and as the United Nations has neither the resources in stock nor an advance budget which would ensure that the required equipment could be made available in a timely manner. It was for this reason that...I underlined [on 13 May] the necessity for Member States to agree to make arrangements on a bilateral basis to provide the troops, equipment and airlift required for UNAMIR. As this did not occur, the Secretariat was required to identify sources of equipment and to arrange for its transport. This was a time-consuming task, which significantly delayed deployment. It also restricted the initial operational capability of UNAMIR, as contingents were in some cases unfamiliar with equipment supplied to them.[72]

Significantly, this fundamental divergence between African needs and Western actions was no less pronounced two years later, concerning Eastern Zaire. In

---

[67] Initially, the UN took advantage of its small observer mission along the Uganda-Rwanda border and used Uganda's main airport in Entebbe to support the operation. See "Third Progress Report of the Secretary-General on the United Nations Observer Mission Uganda-Rwanda," S/1994/1073, 19 September 1994, para.7.

[68] The Council authorized the force on 22 June (see S/RES/929 (1994), 22 June 1994), and it was operational within two weeks. See "Final Report on *Operation Turquoise* Authorized by Security Council Resolution 929 (1994) (Annex)," S/1994/1100, 27 September 1994.

[69] See "Letter dated 1 August 1994 from the Secretary-General to the President of the Security Council reporting his urgent request to Governments to provide the reinforcements and equipment necessary to bring UNAMIR to the strength authorized by the Council in Resolution 918 (1994)," S/1994/923, 3 August 1994.

[70] They were: Ethiopia (800 troops), Ghana (800), Malawi (120), Mali (200), Nigeria (300), Tunisia (600), Zambia (800), and Zimbabwe (800). *Ibid.*

[71] These countries -- all participants in *Operation Turquoise* – were: Chad, Congo, Guinea Bissau, Niger, and Senegal. See S/1994/1100, 27 September 1994, and S/1994/1133, 6 October 1994, para.33. (Egyptian and Mauritanian troops also served in *Operation Turquoise*.) Initially, the new government in Kigali, which assumed control of the capital on 4 July, would not accept troops from any countries participating in the multinational force. See "Report of the Secretary-General on the Situation in Rwanda," S/1994/924, 3 August 1994, para.24.

[72] "Progress Report of the Secretary-General on the United Nations Assistance Mission for Rwanda," S/1994/1133, 6 October 1994, para.35.

November 1996, the Security Council begrudgingly authorized the deployment of a multinational force in Eastern Zaire to facilitate the delivery of humanitarian aid and the voluntary repatriation of refugees.[73] Canada, which had offered to lead the mission, found no shortage of African countries willing to contribute troops.[74] The force never deployed -- ostensibly because the situation resolved itself when thousands of Rwandese refugees returned home. Yet the plans and politics behind the operation highlighted Africa's dependence on the West (in particular, the United States)[75] as well as the perceived Western reluctance to provide the assistance needed.

Limitations of African Approaches

It is not surprising that many of the aforementioned African undertakings have made only a negligible impact. Sub-regional organizations such as AMU, ECCAS, and IGAD possess few decision-making mechanisms in direct support of peace and security. Yet even the initiatives of several of the (relatively) more institutionalized organizations such as the OAU, ECOWAS, and SADC are seriously flawed.

OAU

The OAU still lacks the capacity to conduct credible and effective peacekeeping operations. Its Mechanism has not made a significant impact since it was established in 1993. Only five percent of the OAU's budget is allocated to peace initiatives. The failure of the majority of OAU member states to pay their dues on time and in full exacerbates the problem. The OAU Peace Fund established to help alleviate the Mechanism's financial limitations has been of limited effectiveness. Although the UN and a number of Western states have made significant contributions to the OAU's conflict management machinery,[76] these contributions have not always prompted meaningful results. OAU Military Observer Missions are still dependent on further outside assistance.[77] Moreover, neither the Crisis Management Room

---

[73] See S/RES/1080 (1996), 15 November 1996. The fact that the multinational force was not tasked with disarming returning refugees (who were certain to include ex-FAR and *Interahamwe*) may have hastened Laurent-Desirée Kabila's rebellion and the ensuing civil war.

[74] See "Emergency Update 29 on Eastern Zaire," *UN Department of Humanitarian Affairs Integrated Regional Information Network*, 18 November 1996.

[75] See James Appathurai and Ralph Lysyshyn, "Lessons Learned from the Zaire Mission," *Canadian Foreign Policy*, Vol. 5, No. 2, Winter 1998, pp.99-105.

[76] Canada, France, Japan, the UK, and the US have been among the most generous donors. The US, for example, funded the construction of the Conflict Management Centre and has provided approximately US$ 3 million per year to support the Mechanism. Interview with Bakwesegha, note 31. France pledged US$ 1.2 million to the Mechanism for fiscal year 1998. This money was intended to furnish the Conflict Management Centre as well as to provide transportation and equipment for actual operations. Interview with Digonnet, note 14. See also, Ghion Hagos, "France Pledges Africa One Million Dollars for Security," *Panafrican News Agency*, 10 October 1997.

[77] For example, France provided roughly US$ 300,000 of logistical assistance to the OAU Observer Mission in the Comoros, deployed in December 1997. The French Ministry of Defense "loaned" the Mission a number of vehicles from its Reunion fleet while the Ministry of Cooperation "gave" a number of others. Interview with Digonnet, note 14.

nor the Early Warning Network is fully operational. Throwing more money at the problem is no solution.[78]

The OAU's plan to establish a standby African peacekeeping force is wildly unrealistic. In the past four years, the OAU has deployed only three small observer missions. NMOG I and II had mandated strengths of 50 and 130, respectively. OMIB initially constituted 47 military officers and was subsequently expanded to 67. The Comoros force comprises some 20 observers.[79] Although such missions may play an important symbolic role, they cannot be expected to assume multifaceted peacekeeping operations. Given that the OAU has had to go hat in hand to donors for items such as boots, socks, and flashlights for its mission participants, it is difficult to see how it plans to field OAU missions comprised of sub-regional brigades. Moreover, in light of African countries' lukewarm commitment to the existing UN Standby Arrangements System,[80] the idea seems overly ambitious.[81] Even its request to have 500 military observers identified as a short-term measure is far-fetched.

ECOWAS

ECOMOG proved willing and able to intervene in Liberia, but its assistance actually exacerbated the conflict rather than helped to resolve or manage it. It is true that after receiving additional resources the West African force was somewhat more effective during the year leading up to the July 1997 elections. Yet the entire seven-year period of its involvement in Liberia must be reviewed when judging whether ECOMOG was a success. As concerns Liberia, ECOMOG was a misnomer. Its architects never intended it simply to "monitor" the situation. It was never a neutral force, and it prolonged the conflict. The various factions knew they could count on the support of different ECOWAS member states.

The intervention in Sierra Leone may play a more positive role for that country's and the region's peace and security -- at least in the short term. Reinstating Sierra Leone's democratically-elected president is both defensible and preferable to allowing the junta to run the country further into the ground. A more capable force may well have succeeded in further weakening the retreating junta, but no such force was in the offing.

The longer-term implications of "ECOMOG's" intervention into Sierra Leone are more worrisome and call into question ECOWAS' desire to establish a permanent peacekeeping mechanism. There is growing and justifiable concern that Nigeria

---

[78] A UN official familiar with the issue opined that the OAU's Conflict Management Division needed personnel willing to "roll up their sleeves and work" rather than more money. Interview with Department of Peacekeeping Operations official, New York, 16 March 1998.

[79] Telephone interview with Nhara, note 28.

[80] As of 1 July 1998, 18 African countries had officially expressed their willingness to participate in UN Standby Arrangements. Of those, only Ghana has actually signed a memorandum of understanding with the UN. See Monthly Status Report, UN Standby Arrangements, 1 July 1998.

[81] See Malan, "Towards Sounder Investments in Developing African Peace Operations Capabilities," note 64, p.24.

would manipulate such a force into a tool to further its hegemonic aspirations, much in the same manner as it has hijacked the good name of ECOMOG in Sierra Leone. For all intents and purposes, the ECOMOG force is Nigerian.[82] Nigeria intervened in Sierra Leone without consulting its partners or receiving prior authorization.[83] Referring to it as the "Nigerian-led ECOMOG peacekeeping force" is of incalculable value to a country desiring some good public relations.[84]

SADC

Although the SADC region is undertaking important peacekeeping training initiatives,[85] the Organ itself is not yet functioning. The current controversy surrounds the question of whether the Organ is a subsidiary of SADC or a parallel structure. South Africa maintains that it is a SADC sub-structure and thus argues that both the economic and security issues of the sub-region should be addressed in a single SADC Summit. Zimbabwe asserts that the Organ is an autonomous institution, and thus that there should be two summits -- a SADC Summit devoted to economic issues and an Organ Summit devoted to security issues, under separate chairpersons.[86] While this dispute remains unresolved, the Organ will exist only on paper and its peacekeeping role will remain unknown.[87]

Another important determinant of SADC's peacekeeping potential will be South Africa's future role in the organization.[88] As the most powerful state in the sub-

---

[82] Besides Nigeria, Guinea is the only other ECOWAS member to provide troops, and those troops remained on its soil along the border with Sierra Leone.

[83] See "Putting a country together again," *The Economist*, 21 February 1998, p.48, and "Ironies," *The Economist*, 6 September 1997, p.44.

[84] Thus, while Nigeria complains bitterly about the costs it must shoulder to undertake ECOMOG operations, it is in its self-interest to continue to support these missions. Nevertheless, the loss of a sound and broader financial base limits ECOMOG's effectiveness.

[85] *Blue Hungwe* and the upcoming *Blue Crane* are sub-regional peacekeeping training exercises involving troops from most SADC countries, but they are not organized under SADC auspices.

[86] Interview with Hamman, note 54. Although the issue was referred to Malawi, Mozambique, and Namibia to resolve in March 1998, no conclusion had been reached as of 1 July 1998.

[87] Mark Malan, "SADC and Subregional Security: *Unde Venis et Quo Vadis*," ISS *Monograph Series*, Vol. 19, Halfway House, South Africa: Institute for Security Studies, February 1998, p.17. SADC's peacekeeping capabilities have not been tested. Although the unified response of Botswana, South Africa, and Zimbabwe to the Lesotho crisis in 1994 is often cited as an important example, its precedential value is quite limited. The Lesotho operation took place just after the 1994 elections in South Africa, and was very much an *ad hoc*, FLS-style response. Ultimately, a "show of force" along the Lesotho border was adequate to quell the unrest, and no "peacekeeping" was involved. Interview with Dr. R.M. "Rocky" Williams and Mr. Nick Stendall, Defence Policy Department, South African Department of Defence, Halfway House, South Africa, 23 January 1998.

[88] The fact that South Africa will host *Blue Crane* in October 1998 seemingly attests to its willingness to enhance the sub-region's peacekeeping capabilities. Unlike *Blue Hungwe* and *Guidimakha*, which each had one principal Western supporter, *Blue Crane* will have a number of Western sponsors. Having received numerous capacity-building offers, South Africa assumed that the donor community would readily fund the exercise, which is expected to cost US$ 2.5 million. However, securing Western support has proven exceedingly difficult. The US, for example, would not support *Blue Crane* without linking it to ACRI. See Jakkie Cilliers, "The United States, Southern Africa, the ACRI and the ACSS," *Background Paper Prepared for a Meeting with Amb. Marshall Fletcher McCallie*, April 1998.

region -- both economically and militarily -- South Africa will exert a decisive influence on the sub-region's peacekeeping policy.[89] Presently, South Africa is focusing on its own capabilities and national interests before looking externally.[90] In light of its history, South Africa is also sensitive about appearing as the dominant state in Southern Africa. Should South Africa decide to play a more deterministic role in the sub-region, SADC has the potential to make a positive contribution to African peace and security. Should it not, however, SADC's peacekeeping capacity would be significantly reduced.

Ad Hoc Coalitions

The inter-African peacekeeping force in CAR highlights several of the shortcomings of current African responses. MISAB required the direct assistance of France to deploy and become operational. The force also required French logistical and tactical support on the ground.[91] Although each participating state provided its troops with their regular pay and supplied them with weapons, France paid their total food allowance and daily subsistence allowance at rates then applicable to Central African military personnel. France also supplied, maintained, and provided fuel for tactical and support vehicles, paid rents for buildings used by MISAB command and military personnel, and donated office equipment.[92] France estimated the cost of its support at US$ 2 million per month.[93] No other outside support from UN member states was forthcoming.[94]

The contemplated peacekeeping operation in Congo similarly illustrates the limitations of African actors. Although the Council ultimately decided not to

---

[89] The White Paper on Peacekeeping, which is presently being finalized, will clarify South Africa's approach to peacekeeping.

[90] The South African National Defence Forces are undergoing a significant restructuring. Moreover, its defense budget has declined some 60 percent over the last six years. Interview with Williams and Stendall, note 87.

[91] As Secretary-General Annan noted in his 23 February 1998 Report, "MISAB will not be able to continue its presence in Bangui without external financial and logistical support." "Report of the Secretary-General Pursuant to Resolution 1152 (1998) Concerning the Situation in the Central African Republic," S/1998/148, 23 February 1998, para.20.

[92] See "Letter Dated 20 August 1997 From the Secretary-General Addressed to the President of the Security Council (Enclosure)," S/1997/652, 21 August 1997, containing the International Monitoring Committee's First Report to the Security Council Pursuant to Resolution 1125 (1997).

[93] Interview with Col. Bruno Dary, Director, Operational Center, Africa Division, État Major des Armées, Paris, 29 May 1998.

[94] In Resolution 1136, the Security Council requested the Secretary-General to establish a Trust Fund for CAR. S/RES/1136 (1997), 6 November 1997. This Trust Fund never received any contributions. (Interview with Peter Due, Political Affairs Officer, Department of Peacekeeping Operations, New York, 17 March 1998.) The OAU, however, did provide two grants totalling US$ 100,000. See "Letter Dated 20 August 1997 From the Secretary-General Addressed to the President of the Security Council (Enclosure)," S/1997/652, 21 August 1997, containing the International Monitoring Committee's First Report to the Security Council Pursuant to Resolution 1125 (1997).

authorize such a force, the proposed Senegalese-led force could not have deployed without outside assistance. As the Secretary-General observed in his 21 October 1997 Report to the Security Council: "No country emerged that was able and willing to assure the command, control and communications capacity, the rapid deployment capability or the ability to generate the necessary financing that would be required to assume the leadership of a multinational force."[95] Moreover, according to the Report, "[m]ost potential troop contributors specified that the force should be a United Nations peacekeeping operation rather than a multinational force."[96] This detail is quite significant. UN peacekeeping operations are supported through non-negotiable assessments based largely on contributions to the UN's regular budget with permanent members of the Security Council paying a premium. Multinational forces are financed through voluntary contributions with participants expected to cover their own costs. A number of African countries are unable or unwilling to participate in peace operations that receive Security Council authorization as multinational forces but do not receive UN equipment or financing.[97]

Unresponsiveness of Western Approaches

Western capacity-building efforts do not redress the fundamental limitations of African peacekeepers. Although the needs of African countries are well-known, Western countries are pursuing policies that respond to their own needs. This is neither surprising nor inherently troubling. The problem is that Western interests reflect a marginalization of African peace and security.

ACRI is first and foremost a response to perceived American needs and political realities. It reflects the desire of the US not to be drawn into armed conflicts and humanitarian tragedies in Africa. Indeed, the impetus behind the program was to devise a quick-fix response in mid-1996 to the anticipated bloodbath in Burundi and to avoid having to commit American troops. It also reflects the Clinton Administration's acknowledgment of several restrictive political realities. Many US government officials readily concede that ACRI is flawed. At the same time, however, they stress that it represents the best policy option that can realistically be expected to garner Congressional support.[98] (Isolationist and anti-UN sentiment in Congress does represent a very real constraint -- one that the Administration

---

[95] "Report of the Secretary-General on the Situation in the Republic of Congo," S/1997/814, 21 October 1997, para.27.

[96] *Ibid.*

[97] For example, when the first United Nations Operation in Somalia (UNOSOM I) was transformed into the United Task Force (UNITAF) -- a MNF -- it undermined some African states' resolve to participate. Zimbabwe, which had agreed initially to send an infantry battalion, waited until the Council authorized UNOSOM II to replace UNITAF before completing its deployment.

[98] Interviews with US government officials, Geneva, Johannesburg, and Washington, DC, Winter and Spring 1998.

helped to create[99] -- but it need not be insurmountable.) International support is also limited.[100]

RECAMP, like ACRI, is above all a response to domestic interests and limitations. What is billed as a strengthened commitment to African peacekeeping can best be understood as a cost-cutting measure intended to reduce France's traditional exposure and expenses on the continent. At the instigation of Prime Minister Lionel Jospin, France is scaling down substantially its military presence throughout Africa. In August 1997, the government announced plans to reduce its military forces stationed in Africa by over 30 percent.[101] The collapse of the Cooperation Ministry into the Ministry of Foreign Affairs is a further indication that Africa's privileged status in the formulation of French foreign policy is waning. As France's schizophrenic support for the proposed Senegalese-led operation in Congo[102] and its eagerness to extract itself from MISAB in CAR both attest, its commitment to strengthening peacekeeping on the continent is dubious.

The P-3 and other Western efforts aim to build capabilities, but it is not clear how these capabilities would eventually be used. It has not been determined who would elect to send these trained troops, under whose command they would operate, or how they would be deployed.[103] Western countries may be building a capacity that will never be tapped effectively. Under the terms of the memorandum of understanding that ACRI recipients must sign, they agree only to refrain from using the donated equipment for unintended purposes.[104] They are under no obligation to participate in any eventual force. The enthusiasm of ACRI recipients for the program may have more to do with helping themselves to US training and equipment now than with helping their fellow Africans later.

Such criticisms do not mean that Western capacity-building policies are without value. Additional training has its benefits (although the "classical" peacekeeping

---

[99] The Administration has poisoned public opinion by repeatedly making the UN a scapegoat.

[100] Initially, the US proposed to pay half of the program's anticipated cost with its European allies or the UN making up the rest. (Michela Wrong, "US Moving to Train African Peace Troops," *Financial Times*, 11 October 1998, p.8.) However, no outside funding was forthcoming. The US Congress has agreed to fund ACRI only on an annual basis and has limited its support to some US$ 15 million per year.

[101] The French Minister of Defense, Alain Richard, confirmed that France would reduce its forces from 8,100 to fewer than 6,000, and would close its bases in CAR. See Hugo Sada, "L'allègement du dispositif français en Afrique," *Sommaire - défense nationale*, p.189. See also "France: A New Foreign Policy," *The Economist*, 6 September 1997, p.32.

[102] While France was expressing its tentative support before the Security Council for a UN-authorized intervention, President Jacques Chirac allegedly cut a deal with the opposition on behalf of French business interests. See Baffour Ankomah, "'Chuck your bloody constitution in the dustbin,'" *New African*, May 1998, pp.12-13.

[103] According to Amb. McCallie, these are issues that African countries will decide. Interview with McCallie, note 19.

[104] One of the reasons that Ethiopia's training had initially been delayed had to do with Ethiopia's unhappiness with the terms of the memorandum of understanding. Interview with Ikins, note 22.

training being offered is of limited utility given the likely nature of conflicts in Africa). As a result of ACRI, the issue of African peace and security is higher on the US agenda. France's decision to pre-position equipment together with a willingness to dispense with it for peacekeeping operations has proven beneficial. A much needed dialogue -- especially among France, the UK, and the US concerning their respective activities in Africa -- has begun to take place. The 5 December 1997 meeting in New York and *Guidimakha* are concrete examples of cooperation.

As the recent negotiations behind the establishment of a UN peacekeeping operation in the Central African Republic illustrate, however, a good deal of distrust and competing interests still exists among the Western actors. The Clinton Administration's reluctant and much-delayed support for the UN peacekeeping operation in CAR made the eventual transition to the UN force difficult and acrimonious. It should have been possible to extract additional concessions from France (concerning what assets it would leave behind and make available) and from President Patassé (concerning the domestic opposition and the International Monetary Fund) without resorting to stonewalling. France also exacerbated tensions by withdrawing many of its troops prematurely. American and French actions served neither the interests of Africa nor the international community.

Conclusion

There is little reason to believe that the West has learned from its mistakes and is better prepared to respond meaningfully to crises in Africa. Billed as "engagement" policies, Western capacity-building programs are in fact just the opposite. The Western-driven Security Council will continue to "disengage" from Africa, notwithstanding its responsibility for the maintenance of peace and security. As the difficulties encountered in establishing a UN peacekeeping operation in the Central African Republic evidence, the Council is reluctant to approve of worthwhile UN undertakings in Africa -- even those that are well thought-out and relatively inexpensive.

African actors are thus correct to seek "African solutions to African problems." Yet the responses they have devised are partial at best. The political will of African actors far outstrips their peacekeeping capabilities. In spite of their efforts and initiatives, African countries are not yet in a position to go it alone.

The patchwork of present approaches highlights the inadequacy of the *status quo*. Current talk of "partnerships" between the West and Africa is misleading. African recipients of current Western capacity-building schemes are little more than proxies.

Today, more than four years after the genocide in Rwanda, African countries largely possess the troops and the will to intervene, but not the means. Western countries, for their part, are still pursuing policies that respond primarily to their own needs. African peace and security will continue to be undermined as long as the West views such concerns as divisible from international peace and security.

Glossary of Terms

ACRF	African Crisis Response Force
ACRI	African Crisis Response Initiative
AMU	Arab Maghreb Union
ANAD	Accord de non-aggression et d'assistance en matière de défense (Treaty of Non-Aggression, Assistance, and Mutual Defence)
ASAS	Association of Southern African States
BMATT	British Military Advisory and Training Team
CAR	Central African Republic
CMC	Conflict Management Centre
DRC	Democratic Republic of Congo
EAC	Commission for East African Co-operation
ECCAS	Economic Community of Central African States
ECOMOG	ECOWAS Cease-fire Monitoring Group
ECOWAS	Economic Community of West African States
FLS	Front Line States
IGAD	Inter-Governmental Authority on Development
IGADD	Inter-Governmental Authority on Drought and Development
ISDSC	Inter-State Defence and Security Committee
MINURCA	United Nations Mission in the Central African Republic
MISAB	Mission interafricaine de surveillance des accords de Bangui (Inter-African Mission to Monitor the Implementation of the Bangui Agreements)
NMOG	Neutral Military Observer Group
OAU	Organization of African Unity
OMIB	Observer Mission in Burundi
RECAMP	Renforcement des capacités africaines de maintain de la paix
SADC	Southern African Development Community
SADCC	Southern African Development Co-ordination Conference
UNAMIR	United Nations Assistance Mission for Rwanda
UNITAF	United Task Force
UNOSOM	United Nations Operation in Somalia

The Lester B. Pearson Canadian International Peacekeeping Training Centre

Le centre canadien international Lester B. Pearson pour la formation en maintien de la paix

THE PEARSON PEACEKEEPING CENTRE AND THE NEW PEACEKEEPING PARTNERSHIP

The mission of the Lester B. Pearson Canadian International Peacekeeping Centre is to provide national and international participants with the opportunity to examine specific peacekeeping issues and to update their knowledge of the latest peacekeeping practices. To guide its activities, the PPC has developed the concept of the **New Peacekeeping Partnership**, the term applied to those organizations and individuals that work together to improve the effectiveness of modern peacekeeping operations. It includes: the military; civil police; government, and non-government agencies dealing with human rights and humanitarian assistance; diplomats; the media; and organizations sponsoring development and democratization programmes.

The Pearson Peacekeeping Centre offers a multifaceted curriculum of special interest to all the stakeholders associated with peacekeeping operations, through an extensive schedule of conferences, seminars, workshops, training and educational courses. Off-campus activities are conducted by mobile training teams or through electronic distant-learning technology.

The Centre also sponsors field research with deployed peacekeeping missions and a Visiting Scholar Programme. Researchers in any peacekeeping-related discipline can arrange for access to the Centre's archives. In addition to its scheduled functions, the Centre has the ability to respond quickly to requests for specialized research or customized training packages. It also functions as an information clearing house and research centre and its multidisciplinary approach reflects the changes in the international environment and "The Changing Face of Peacekeeping". The Centre also conducts a sizeable and active internship programme which allows students to gain valuable working experience while learning more about peacekeeping.

For more information on the Pearson Peacekeeping Centre's programmes, activities and publications, please contact:

Alex Morrison, President, The Pearson Peacekeeping Centre
Cornwallis Park, PO Box 100, Clementsport, NS B0S 1E0 CANADA
Tel: (902) 638-8041 Fax: (902) 638-3344
Email: amorriso@ppc.cdnpeacekeeping.ns.ca
Website: http://www.cdnpeacekeeping.ns.ca

The Pearson Peacekeeping Centre is named in honour of Lester B. Pearson, former Prime Minister of Canada. In 1956, at the time of the Suez Crisis, he invented peacekeeping for which he was awarded the 1957 Nobel Peace Prize.

The Centre (a division of the Canadian Institute of Strategic Studies), established by the Government of Canada in 1994, is funded, in part, by the Department of Foreign Affairs and International Trade and the Department of National Defence of Canada.
Le Centre (une division de l'Institut canadien d'études stratégiques) a été établi par le Gouvernement du Canada en 1994. Le soutien financier du Centre provient, en partie, des ministères des Affaires étrangères et du commerce international et de la défense nationale.

THE CANADIAN PEACEKEEPING PRESS

The Canadian Peacekeeping Press, the publishing arm of the Pearson Peacekeeping Centre, has a number of publications of interest. These include: *UN Peace Operations and the Role of Japan* (edited by Alex Morrison and James Kiras, softcover, 123 pp., $20 + taxes and shipping); *Facing the Future: Proceedings of the 1996 Canada-Japan Conference on Modern Peacekeeping* (edited by Alex Morrison, Ken Eyre and Roger Chiasson, softcover, 222 pp., $20 + GST and shipping); and *Seeds of Freedom: Personal Reflections on the Dawning of Democracy* (by Senator Al Graham, softcover, 288 pp., $30 + taxes and shipping).

Recent publications of the Canadian Peacekeeping Press include: *Theory, Doctrine and Practice of Conflict De-escalation in Peacekeeping Operations* (by David Last, softcover, 152 pp., $23.50 + taxes and shipping); *Refugees, Resources and Resoluteness* (edited by Alex Morrison, Stephanie A. Blair and Dale Anderson, softcover, 186 pp., $20 + GST and shipping); and *Multilateralism and Regional Security* (edited by Michel Fortmann, S. Neil MacFarlane and Stéphane Roussel, softcover, 262 pp., $23.50 + taxes and shipping).

To obtain a Publications Catalogue or for more information on the Canadian Peacekeeping Press, please contact:

Sue Armstrong
Publications Manager
Pearson Peacekeeping Centre
Cornwallis Park, PO Box 100
Clementsport, NS B0S 1E0
Tel: (902) 638-8611 x 161
Fax: (902) 638-8576
Email: sarmstro@ppc.cdnpeacekeeping.ns.ca
Website: http://www.cdnpeacekeeping.ns.ca

The Centre (a division of the Canadian Institute of Strategic Studies), established by the Government of Canada in 1994, is funded, in part, by the Department of Foreign Affairs and International Trade and the Department of National Defence of Canada.
Le Centre (une division de l'Institut canadien d'études stratégiques) a été établi par le Gouvernement du Canada en 1994. Le soutien financier du Centre provient, en partie, des ministères des Affaires étrangères et du commerce international et de la défense nationale.